My Seven Cats

Heidemarie Wawrzyn

My Seven Cats

Bibliografische Information der Deutschen Nationalbibliothek:
Die Deutsche Nationalbibliothek verzeichnet diese Publikation in der
Deutschen Nationalbibliografie; detaillierte bibliografische Daten
sind im Internet über http://dnb.dnb.de abrufbar.

Herstellung und Verlag:
BoD - Books on Demand, Norderstedt, Germany

ISBN: 9783751967372

To Liam

Table of Contents

About the Author   - - -   8

Preface:

Right from the Cats' Mind - - - 10

My Buddha Cat   - - -   17

Little Snowflake   - - -   19

Mom Cat Imi   - - -   23

Cat Pamuk   - - -   27

My Socrates   - - -   29

Cat Mascara   - - -   31

My Good Old Fritz   - - -   35

Postscript   - - -   38

Photos:

Short Notes   - - -   41

About the Author

Heidemarie Wawrzyn grew up in Berlin and studied History of Religions at the University of Bremen. In 1998, she received a doctorate degree for her research on antisemitism in the early German women's movement.

A few months later, in 1999, she moved to Jerusalem, where she worked at different German and Jewish institutes. She became a postdoctoral researcher at the Hebrew University of Jerusalem in 2001 and a freelance transcriber of old German handwritten documents. Until her retirement in 2016, she was employed by the L. A. Mayer Museum for Islamic Art in Jerusalem.

During her years in Jerusalem, the writer gradually turned into a great cat lover. This is probably not a big surprise for those who know

Jerusalem, which has one of the largest stray-cat populations in the world. Generally, many residents here are happy to feed the cats. They may not always invite them into their homes, but they will certainly make sure that street cats are well fed.* The author is one of them.

"My Seven Cats" is the author's fourth collection of poems, which mirrors her special relationship with felines and invites the reader to learn from them.*

Jerusalem, June 2020

*https://aardvarkisrael.com/cats-in-israel/ (June 30, 2020).

Preface:
Right from the Cats' Mind

A few years ago, I walked through the streets of Charlottenburg, a district of Berlin. Since I was there as a tourist with lots of free time on my hands, I strolled from one little, interesting store to the next. In a small stationery shop, a postcard with a beautiful cat caught my eye. On the bottom of the card, you could read the following words: "God created the cat so that man [woman] has a tiger to pet." The text made me smile. I liked this idea and asked myself what I actually love about cats.

Cats like quiet. They walk on soft, silent paws. Noise scares them and makes them run off. They seem to enjoy the good calm moments of life. Watch them, when they eat something yummy, or when they sleep, or enjoy the warm sun after a long harsh winter. Only the moment seems to count, which they deeply enjoy.

Sometimes, cats radiate equanimity and inner peace. One of my felines shows a great deal of serenity in almost every situation. Thus, I often call her my Buddha Cat. She displays inner calmness whatever happens around her – as if she wants to tell me, "Everything in life comes and goes, appears and disappears like a never-ending cycle. Accept the way of life as it is."

Cats do not complain when they are sick. They just withdraw themselves from their home and hide somewhere else, accepting the situation as it is. Only when the worst is over, do they return. However, there are some cats, who come to me because they feel miserable. There is no complaining either, just a mute appearance at my door and hope in their eyes that I might perhaps help them to get better.

Furthermore, it is heartwarming to watch female cats taking care of their kittens. A mother cat protects and nurses her newborn day in, day out. She cleans them and carries them to safe places to give them a protected home. She searches for them when they get lost. She fulfills all these tasks even if she is tired, exhausted or sick. She shows them how to keep themselves clean, how to fight and protect themselves and to pay great attention to the traffic on the street. She teaches them to survive in our world.

It is possible to bond with a cat and communicate without words. It is also possible to sense how a cat feels and vice versa. Some cats are so-called medical cats. They come to you when you are in pain or feel very sad. They jump on your lap and start purring, which can be very relaxing and restorative.

What do I love the most about cats? Their independence and strong will. Most of the cats like to be free and independent. They only do what they want to do. It is almost impossible to force them to something they do not want to do. Cats are not submissive; they love to be free.

My „Buddha Cat"

When I met you sitting on my doorstep,
You had already gone through many pregnancies.
You looked skinny, exhausted, out of energy.

When you disappeared for two or three days,
I was worried and assumed you had left for good.
But you showed up again – spayed and alive!

When I met you sitting on my doorstep for the third time,
I offered you a temporary home; you moved in for good.
I started calling you "Aurora," the Goddess of the Dawn.

Your white fur with its big yellow and golden spots
Brightened my sometimes-lonely and moody hours.
Our rocky communication improved from day to day.

Years went by and I got totally used to your presence.
Your slow way of moving and majestic way of sitting
Make me see and feel your inner serenity.

You are my "Buddha Cat".

Little Snowflake

When I saw you for the first time,
You were a well-developed, middle-sized kitten,
Cute face, white fur with big black spots on your back;
One of them was special; it looked like a heart.

Every day you showed up in my little courtyard.
I started feeding you and opening my heart to you.
As the days went by, you gradually moved into my house.
Each day, you seemed to feel more comfortable and at ease.

At nighttime, you loved to sleep next to me.
Every night you moved a bit closer to me,
Sometimes you cuddled your face next to my shoulder.
You purred deeply and peacefully: Music to my ears.

Then, all of a sudden, you developed a food allergy.

The vet could not help; pills and ointments failed.

Once you ached so much that I was close to tears.

Your pain and suffering was heartbreaking.

Little Snowflake, you became my hero.

You never complained; you never gave up.

At bad times, you withdrew into a neighboring garden.

At better times, you spent the entire day sleeping at home.

Changing your food and cooling your itchy spots

Were the remedies you accepted without any complaint.

Slowly, slowly your health improved.

You returned to being the cat I had known before:

The cat with the great heart.

Mom Cat Imi

Day after day, a tricolored cat knocked at my door for food.
One day, she looked a bit pregnant and each day a bit more.
Then the exciting day came:
On July 4, she gave birth in a nearby garden.

Mom Imi*, you took good care of your four tiny babies.
You searched for them when they went missing.
You looked for them in every corner of the garden.
You kept calling them until they were back with you.

One day, you were sick and had to spend a night at home.
However, you longed for your babies and sneaked out.
Next morning, I found you reunited with your kittens.
What a lovely pack: cute, frisky, embracing the moment!

* Hebrew = my mother

Once, after a heavy rainfall, one kitten was missing.

You searched for him many days in a row.

One time, you even took a piece of chicken with you.

Watching your pure love was touching and heartbreaking.

However, as soon as your time as a caring mom ended,

You returned to your daily life and former hiding place,

Knowing that your children will make it.

You had taught them everything they needed to know

to survive.

Thank you, Imi!

Cat Pamuk

Cat Pamuk has his own special ways:
He does not purr. Instead, he squeaks.
He squeaks for food and attention.
He peeps to say hello or goodbye.

He loves to sleep high up on my gallery,
Hiding at night from other cats and me.
In the morning, he sits at the edge of the loft
To send his early cute squeaks down to me.

Sometimes he looks straight into my eyes,
As if he can read my thoughts and feelings.
There is no blinking, no fear, only trust and good will.
You make me feel like a good, close friend.

Thank you, my lovely Pamuk.

You are My Socrates

You were born on a special day – July 4.

As soon as I saw you, I fell in love with you,

Especially with your light green eyes.

They seemed to be full of light and wisdom.

I whispered, "You are my Socrates."

Your mom brought you and your siblings to my doorstep.

You were the one who trusted me immediately.

You allowed me to pet your white, soft fur.

When I cuddled you, my eyes met yours.

I whispered, "You are my Socrates."

You developed into a beautiful, independent cat.

A few times a day, you show up at my door.

You still allow me to pet your back and your belly.

Whenever our eyes meet each other,

I still whisper, "You are my Socrates."

Cat Mascara

Mascara, your siblings are Pamuk and Socrates,
Your great loving mother is Imi.
You look like your mom; \
You have the same tricolored fur as her.

Mascara, you have very special eyes:
A big black ring surrounds them.
Before I could even come up with a name for you,
Neighbors and friends started calling you Mascara.

Mascara, you developed into a gentle, delicate feline.
You are a home cat and an outdoor cat at the same time.
You seem to enjoy both ways of life equally.
This makes you different from your pack.

Mascara, when you decide to sleep in my home,

You love to lay down in a tiny white drawer.

When I accidentally lock you out, you protest so noisily

That you wake up the entire neighborhood.

Mascara, only recently, you allowed me to pet you.

I was surprised how soft and silky your fur felt.

A stream of joy ran through my body.

Thank you for this special moment, my sweet cat.

My Good Old Fritz

I have known you for more than eight years.
One day, you showed up in my garden.
Slowly, slowly you moved into my apartment.

You easily became friends with my two other cats.
After a short time, you allowed me to pet you.
Slowly, slowly a beautiful bond established between us.

Many years went by; you became more independent.
Sometimes I saw you in a park, sometimes on the street.
Slowly, slowly you disappeared into the nearby gardens.

Now, whenever I see you, I promise to be there for you.
Your eyes and body language tell me how you feel.
Slowly, slowly I learned to read that language.

Over a time span, you turned into an admirable senior.
The time will come when you have to leave our globe.
Slowly, slowly I am accepting this aspect of your life.

I will always be there for you, my dear aging Fritz.

Postscript

Eventually our beloved cats turn into seniors. They become older, slower, and weaker and life seems not as enjoyable to them as it was before. However, when I watch aging cats, I often have the impression they are willing to accept the last phase of life as it is. I often sense with them a kind of agreement to go the path of life to the very end. They do it with great dignity and seem to be free of fear. They know or feel – better than us – what it means to be part of a never-ending cycle of life.

In memory of one of my senior cats.

Photos:

Short Notes:

All images were taken from the author's private photo collection.

The photo collage on page 37 includes street and neighbor cats.

Further Booklets of Poetry by

Heidemarie Wawrzyn

Moments of Reflection,
BoD, Books on Demand, Norderstedt, 2019.

Life, Love and Beyond,
BoD, Books on Demand, Norderstedt, 2019.

Mein Dichterland. Gedichte aus Israel,
BoD, Books on Demand, Norderstedt, 2019.